The Craft of Writing

**Marshall Cavendish
Benchmark
New York**

Poetry

MARK MUSSARI

Other Marshall Cavendish Offices:
Marshall Cavendish International (Asia) Private Limited, 1 New Industrial Road, Singapore 536196 • Marshall Cavendish International (Thailand) Co Ltd. 253 Asoke, 12th Flr, Sukhumvit 21 Road, Klongtoey Nua, Wattana, Bangkok 10110, Thailand • Marshall Cavendish (Malaysia) Sdn Bhd, Times Subang, Lot 46, Subang Hi-Tech Industrial Park, Batu Tiga, 40000 Shah Alam, Selangor Darul Ehsan, Malaysia

Marshall Cavendish is a trademark of Times Publishing Limited

All websites were available and accurate when this book was sent to press.

For list of permissions, see page 95.

Library of Congress Cataloging-in-Publication Data
Mussari, Mark. • Poetry / Mark Mussari. • p. cm.—(The craft of writing)
Includes bibliographical references and index. • Summary: "Explores and explains the craft of writing poetry by providing examples and exercises"—Provided by publisher.
ISBN 978-1-60870-500-9 (Print) • ISBN 978-1-60870-652-5 (eBook)
1. Poetry—Juvenile literature. • I. Title. • PN1031.M885 2011 • 808.1—dc22 • 2010042468

Publisher: Michelle Bisson • Art Director: Anahid Hamparian
Series Designer: Alicia Mikles • Photo research by Lindsay Aveilhe

The photographs in this book are used by permission and through the courtesy of:
iStockphoto: cover; iStockphoto: p. 1; Owain Kirby/Getty Images: p. 4; Homer (oil over pencil on paper), Walcot, William (1874-1943)/Private Collection/Photo © The Fine Art Society, London, UK/ The Bridgeman Art Library International: p. 8; The Granger Collection, NYC: p. 11, 14; English School, (20th century)/Private Collection/© Look and Learn/The Bridgeman Art Library International: p. 16; Charles Gatewood/The Image Works: p. 19; Daniel Hulshizer/AP Photo: p.20; The Print Collector/ Heritage/The Image Works: p. 24; The Granger Collection, NYC: p. 27; Asian Art & Archaeology, Inc./ Corbis: p. 33; The Granger Collection, NYC : p. 41; William Blake, Bruce, Ralph (20th century)/Private Collection/© Look and Learn/The Bridgeman Art Library International: p. 43; The Granger Collection, NYC: p. 49, 51, 60; Tony Celentano: p. 61; The Granger Collection, NYC: p. 66; Media Bakery: p. 68; Ruth Gwily, www.ruthgwily.com: p. 72; Archivio GBB/Contrasto/Redux: p. 78.

Printed in Malaysia (T)
135642

Contents

You don't have to be Shakespeare to write poetry—you just need to want to express your thoughts and feelings, and be open to learning the craft.

Introduction

"POETRY IS SIMPLY THE MOST BEAUTIFUL, impressive, and widely effective mode of saying things." That's how the nineteenth-century English poet Matthew Arnold once defined poetry. It may come as a surprise, but poetry has been crafted by people of all ages, in all countries, since ancient times.

Most people think of poetry as something they had to study in school—and many do not recall that experience fondly. Yet, every day people experience some form of poetry. In fact, poetry is difficult to avoid. It may be a song lyric listened to on an iPod or a car radio or in a store. It may be the few lines appearing on a greeting card just purchased for a friend or family member. It may even be a bawdy limerick discovered on a bathroom wall.

Sometimes the poets we study in school seem light years removed from these mundane forms of poetry. When we think of Shakespeare or William Blake or

Emily Dickinson, we conjure up images of serious writers who composed poetry so that English teachers could force it onto unsuspecting students. Yet, nothing could be further from the truth.

Poets write first and foremost to express themselves. They often choose the poetic form because, unlike a novel or a short story, a poem is meant to be heard as well as read. Its sound is often as important as meaning. And in that sound the heart and the mind can speak in ways they cannot in other written forms. When the nineteenth-century American poet Emily Dickinson wrote, her solitary heart found a means of personal expression. In fact, she didn't even want anyone to read most of her poems and had asked that they be burned after her death. Fortunately for the world, they were not destroyed.

For many professional and aspiring writers, poetry offers the best form for expressing thoughts or feelings. The Irish poet William Butler Yeats used poetry to write about such diverse subjects as revolution, aging, and unrequited love. He once described the "stitching and unstitching" that goes into writing a poem, a reference to the writing and rewriting that create good poetry. He added that—on top of all that work—poetry must still seem easy and natural.

People are drawn to poetry, as they are to most art forms, mostly because it brings pleasure. Its condensed language speaks directly to the heart. It conjures up emotions, attracts lovers, infuriates enemies, and evokes laughter and tears—and often in a few words or lines.

To write poetry is to move the heart. Many people are secret poets. They write poetry but are afraid to show it to anyone. This book should help them come out of the closet. After all, as the American poet and philosopher Ralph Waldo Emerson once observed, "All men are poets at heart." And women, as well!

At some point, every schoolchild studies the *Odyssey* and the *Iliad*, two epic poems by Homer.

A Brief History of Poetry

WE'LL PROBABLY NEVER KNOW WHEN THE first poem was composed. Since the oral tradition long precedes the written, the first poem has disappeared. Historians believe that early societies used poetry as a way to record cultural events as well as to tell stories. The world's oldest surviving poem, the *Epic of Gilgamesh*, was written on clay tablets around 2000 BCE in ancient Mesopotamia. It consists of a collection of stories about the mythical hero-king Gilgamesh and his quest for immortality.

In his *Poetics*, the ancient Greek philosopher Aristotle (384–322 BCE) separated poetry into three categories, or genres: epic, comic, and tragic. The word *poetry*, in fact, comes from the Greek word *poesis*, meaning "to make." Modern readers must understand that even the ancient Greek tragic and comic plays were written in verse, often with sections written to be sung by a chorus. From its earliest beginnings, poetry was meant to be *heard!*

Epic Beginnings

An epic poem is a long poem written in a formal style that tells the story of a heroic figure. Most early traditional epics were based on oral poems, usually about a tribal or national hero. In these epics, the fate of a tribe or nation often depends on the hero's actions. Famous epic poems include Homer's *Iliad* and *Odyssey* (late eighth century BCE), the Anglo-Saxon epic *Beowulf* (composed between 700 and 1000 CE), and the twelfth-century French epic *Song of Roland*.

After *Gilgamesh*, the oldest traditional epic poems are Homer's *Iliad* and *Odyssey*, composed some time in the late eighth century BCE. Other poems dating from ancient times include the sacred Indian texts *Ramayana* (dating from between 200 BCE and 200 CE) and *Mahabharata* (written down between 400 BCE and 200 CE). The Tibetan *Epic of Gesar*, one of the longest literary works ever written, is believed to be more than a thousand years old. Yes, poetry has a long and influential history!

Literary epics were written by individual poets in imitation of traditional epic poems. These include the Roman poet Virgil's *Aeneid* (first century BCE) and the seventeenth-century British poet John Milton's *Paradise Lost* (1667).

In this engraving based on John Milton's epic poem, *Paradise Lost,* the archangel Michael is shown expelling Satan from Heaven.

Ancient Love

It may sound like a telephone number, but the world's oldest known love poem is called "Istanbul 2461." The more than four-thousand-year-old poem was discovered in the 1880s on a tablet in Nappur (an area that is now part of Iraq). In this rather risqué love poem, a priestess openly professes her love for a king. The priestess then boldly asks the king to take her to his bedroom.

The *Aeneid*, written in Latin, tells the story of Aeneas, one of the heroes of the Trojan War, as he struggles to make his way home. The subject of *Paradise Lost* is no less than the fall of humankind, including the battle between Satan and God for humanity's soul. Weighty stuff!

English Poetry— a Crash Course

As you can see, poetry had very early beginnings in the history of humanity. Since then, poetry has been written, spoken, or performed in some form in most cultures around the world. Let's focus on some high points in the history of poetry written in the English language.

One of the first great English poets was Geoffrey Chaucer (circa 1342–1400), the author of *Canterbury Tales*, which scholars believe was composed in the late 1300s. Like the early epic writers, Chaucer used the poetic form to tell a series of stories: his narrators are a group of characters going on a religious pilgrimage. He was also one of the first writers to use the vernacular (or everyday language) in his poetry, establishing an important trend in English poetry.

More than four hundred years after his death in 1616, William Shakespeare (born 1564) is still considered by many to be the greatest poet of the English language. Throughout his plays and sonnets, he elevated the English language to a new level of expression, and he infused his verses with every imaginable form of figurative language.

This woodcut from William Caxton's second edition of Chaucer's *Canterbury Tales*, c. 1484, is a rendition of the tale, "Pilgrims at Table."

Remember that Shakespeare wrote at a time when educated writers relied heavily on classical figures of speech (in the tradition of ancient Greece and Rome).

Isn't It Romantic?

In the late-eighteenth and early-nineteenth centuries, a group of poets wanted to revolutionize and reenergize English poetry. They became known as the Romantics —but the word has nothing to do with romance in this usage. Two of these poets, William Wordsworth and Samuel Taylor Coleridge, expressed their thoughts about

Shakespeare, the Poet

It may come as a surprise, but Shakespeare was most famous in his lifetime for a poem, not for his plays (which were also written predominantly in verse or poetic form). *Venus and Adonis*, a narrative poem told in nineteen stanzas (or sections) of six lines each, was printed in 1593. Shakespeare based this poem on the myth of the Roman goddess of love, Venus, and her passion for the youthful Adonis. He took his inspiration from stories in the ancient Roman poet Ovid's *Metamorphoses*. Literature can inspire other literature!

William Wordsworth's sister, Dorothy, was the inspiration for many of his poems.

this "new poetry" in a joint collection of poems titled *Lyrical Ballads*, which appeared in 1798.

In his preface to the *Lyrical Ballads*, Wordsworth called poetry "the spontaneous overflow of powerful feelings." Along with Wordsworth and Coleridge, the major Romantic poets include William Blake, Lord Byron, Percy Bysshe Shelley, and John Keats. Individual creative expression became a major concern of these poets. A strong connection exists between the Romantic poets and their interest in human emotion and more recent poets and their sometimes direct expression of feelings. To this day, the Romantics remain some of the most popular poets in the world.

Open Your Eyes— and Mind!

The Romantic poet and illustrator William Blake (1757–1827) believed that the imaginative person could discover eternity in life's moments. Good advice for aspiring poets? Consider Blake's brief poem entitled, aptly enough, "Eternity":

> He who binds to himself a joy
>
> Does the winged life destroy;
>
> But he who kisses the joy as it flies
>
> Lives in eternity's sunrise.

Poetry

Whitman and Dickinson

In the nineteenth century, two Americans revolutionized the poetic form in markedly different ways. Walt Whitman blew the roof off structured poetry by introducing free verse—poems of irregular line lengths that follow no specific rhyme scheme. Meanwhile, Emily Dickinson began to experiment with rhyme and punctuation: she often employed slant rhyme, rhyme that is not quite exact.

Modern Poetry

Since the early twentieth century, poets, experimenting with a number of forms, have produced some of the most creative and challenging poetry ever written. The image took center stage in the beginning of the twentieth century, and in many ways it has never let go. Belief in the power of the image prompted a school of poets called the Imagists, which included the Americans Ezra Pound; Hilda Doolittle, or H. D.; and Amy Lowell.

The American-born British poet T. S. Eliot is widely considered the father of literary Modernism, and his poem "The Waste Land" (1922) is regarded as one of the most inventive in the English language. Another American poet, Wallace Stevens, believed in the power of the imagination and created experimental poems that sometimes reflected modern movements in art (such as Cubism). The visual aspect of poetry remains one of its strongest attractions.

In more recent times, writers have used poetry to address such diverse topics as race, AIDS, the environment, and nuclear proliferation. And, of course, they are still writing love poems—and probably always will.

Poet and activist Allen Ginsberg was one of a group of Beat poets who demolished the notion that poets were ethereal creatures who did not interact with the real world.

They Had the Beat

Influenced by William Blake and Walt Whitman, the Beat poets were a group of American writers who gathered in New York and San Francisco in the 1950s. Anticonformists who wrote openly about such topics as drugs and sex, the Beats included Allen Ginsberg, Jack Kerouac, and William S. Burroughs. Ginsberg's first collection of poetry, *Howl and Other Poems* (1956), created such a controversy that the book was banned by the U.S. Customs Office!

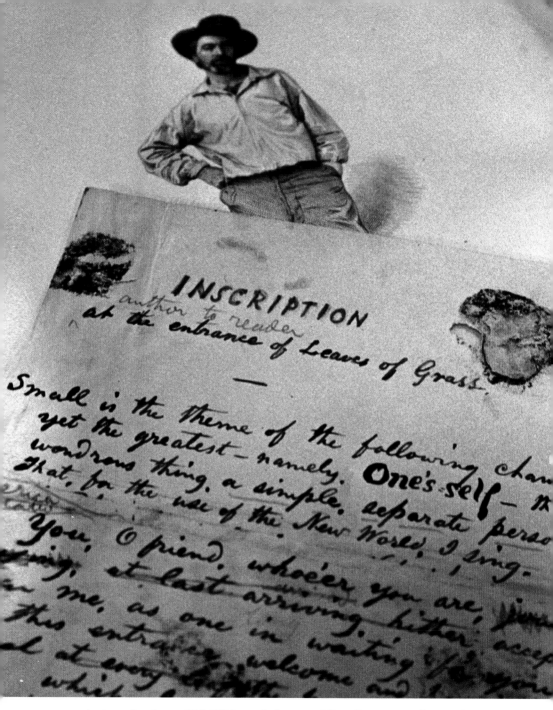

INSCRIPTION
author to reader
at the entrance of Leaves of Grass

Small is the theme of the following chant,
yet the greatest—namely, One's-self—
wondrous thing, a simple, separate person,
That, for the use of the New World, I sing.

You, O friend, whoe'er you are
me, as one in waiting
this entrance, welcome
which

An introduction to Walt Whitman's *Leaves of Grass* lies next to the poet's engraving in this rare first edition of the book found by a professor 130 years after it was written.

2

Types of Poetry

FROM THE JAPANESE HAIKU TO THE SONNET and free verse, anyone wishing to write poetry will find a cornucopia of styles and approaches from which to choose. When thinking about writing a poem, it is always wise to consider the form of the poem. If you read a lot of poems— always a smart idea if you want to become a poet—you'll notice a strong connection between form and subject matter.

Poets often choose certain formats because they are the most effective for what the poet wants to say. There are many poetic forms from which to choose. Most involve a certain number of lines or a specific meter (or rhythm). Many have set rhyme schemes, whereas others are open. And many have no rhyme scheme at all. It is a popular misconception that poems must rhyme.

Ever since Whitman instituted free verse, poets have felt able to write in any form they choose—even to invent new forms. Let's take a look at two specific types of poetry, the sonnet and the haiku, and at the ever-popular free verse. The first is seemingly demanding and the second seemingly simplistic—and free verse seems to say, "Anything goes." But looks are deceiving.

The Sonnet

Consider the sonnet. Many people associate the sonnet with Shakespeare, who certainly excelled at the form, having composed 154 of them sometime late in the sixteenth century. In fact, he was so good at the sonnet form that scholars named the English version after him: the Shakespearean sonnet. You'll really know you've made it as a poet when they name a poetic form after you.

Actually, the sonnet had been around for centuries before Shakespeare. It dates back to the thirteenth and fourteenth centuries, when the Italian poets Dante (1265–1321) and Petrarch (1304–1374) decided to try their hand at it. The prolific Petrarch composed about three hundred or so of the poems. Petrarch was quite successful at the form—he had an adjective named after his style as well: the Italian sonnet is also called the Petrarchan sonnet.

What motivated Petrarch to write all those sonnets? Hint: it begins with the letter "L." Petrarch wrote all of his sonnets to a beautiful woman named Laura, whom he loved and who died young. The object of Dante's sonnets—Beatrice, another beautiful, idealized woman—also died young. Therefore, in its history, the sonnet form became associated with idealized, unrequited (unreturned) love.

Sonnet Style

The sonnet is a poem consisting of fourteen lines with a fixed pattern of rhyme and meter (or stressed beats). In sonnets written in English, each line usually consists of ten syllables of iambic pentameter (five stressed beats, starting with the unstressed syllable). Rhyme schemes have varied since Shakespeare's time, but the English sonnet usually follows this scheme: *abab cdcd efef gg.* Each letter represents a new sound.

Petrarch addressed all of his poems to Laura, a beautiful young woman who died at an early age.

Shakespeare wrote sonnets to a young man and to a mysterious Dark Lady. In the nineteenth century, Words-worth and Keats wrote sonnets about subjects as diverse as nature, death, and ancient Greek statues. By the twentieth century, the sonnet became a favorite form of the American Confessional poets, who used it to express their innermost feelings.

"Bright Star" — a Sonnet and a Movie!

The English poet John Keats (1795–1821) may have been the original "emo" (Emo refers to a somewhat melodramatic, emotional form of music growing out of punk rock and to those who appreciate it). Keats's beautiful and haunting sonnet "Bright Star," written when he was twenty-four, captures his youthful concerns about the passing of time. That sonnet and the poet's tragic life—he died at the age of twenty-six of tuberculosis—inspired a film about him: *Bright Star*, produced in 2009. Here's the sonnet (and you can rent the movie!):

Bright star! Would I were as steadfast as thou art—

Not in lone splendour hung aloft the night

And watching, with eternal lids apart,

Like nature's patient, sleepless eremite,

The moving waters at their priestlike task

Of pure ablution round the earth's human shores,

Or gazing on the new soft-fallen mask

Of snow upon the mountains and the moors;

No—yet still steadfast, still unchangeable,

Pillowed upon my fair love's ripening breast,

To feel for ever its soft fall and swell,

Awake for ever in a sweet unrest,

Still, still to hear her tender-taken breath,

And so live ever—or else swoon to death.

If we look closely at Keats's sonnet "Bright Star," we can see how the type of poem we choose to write can more powerfully reflect its message. Keats chose the Italian form of the sonnet, in which one thought is expressed through the first eight lines, and then a break occurs (called a caesura)—in this case indicated by a semicolon—before the last six lines offer a response or another view.

One of the best-known of Keats's poems is "Ode to a Nightingale." In this oil painting by Joseph Severn in 1845 he is pictured as listening to one such bird in the woods.

27

At the beginning of his sonnet, Keats addresses the star as if it were alive—in poetry addressing an inanimate object in this way is called apostrophe—and tells it that he wishes he were "as steadfast" as it is—but not alone. He carries this thought through the first eight lines in pictures or images of what the solitary star might see: the shoreline, the new-fallen snow. In line nine Keats says, "No, not like that but like this," and proceeds to offer romantic images of human contact. Even though all these images involve the inevitability of time, Keats expresses his longing to feel them permanently. He says he wants to live this way for "ever," as the poem ends on a note of "death."

Keats has used the sonnet form to contrast lonely images of nature in the first eight lines with specific images of passion in the last six lines. His sonnet is a lesson in using concrete images to express ideas or feelings.

Take a look at Dick Allen's modern sonnet "Lost Love," which appeared in the *New Yorker* magazine in 1987. If you count the syllables in each line (go ahead—it's fun), you'll notice that Allen does not adhere to the standard English format of ten syllables to a line. And as far as the rhyme scheme goes, there isn't any until line 9, and then it's: *ababcc*. It looks like a sonnet, though, and it certainly feels like a sonnet. Well, at least it has fourteen lines.

Allen has found an inventive way to use the form in a modern manner. Are there similarities to the standard form? Note that, as in Keats's Italianate sonnet "Bright Star," there's a turnaround at line 9: "But I'm lying." Also, like the speaker in "Bright Star," the speaker in "Lost

Modern Sonnet—"Lost Love"

In case you're wondering, the sonnet form has never died. Here's a contemporary sonnet by Dick Allen on one of the form's favorite themes, lost love:

You're in the city, somewhere. I suppose if I stood

On Times Square a year or two I'd find you,

Face pleasant and older, coming out of the subway crowd,

Or studying poinsettias in a florist's window.

A flicker—that would be all. Both of us

Looked so much like others, which of us could be sure

We were not others? Once, we met in a glance.

So, too, in a glance, should both of us disappear.

But I'm lying. Often, on West Coast or East,

I'll be at a movie before the lights go down

And Beauty flees through the meadows from the Beast

Or the boy steps out of a throng to claim his crown

When far down the aisle and rows I'll see you there,

Your body still young, your eyes, your taffeta hair!

Love" begins saying one thing and then shifts gears after the break. More importantly, look at the images: like Keats, Allen also uses a lot of visual imagery to convey his feelings. You're on a busy city street at one moment—and the next you're in a movie theater.

Why Sonnets?

We may scratch our heads and wonder why modern poets—who have many forms to choose from—would choose the sonnet. Like most poems, the sonnet is both an artistic and a mental exercise. Writing one demands that you concentrate your efforts, that you make your ideas fit a small space.

In many ways, that limitation reflects the strength of much poetry: the language is condensed and, therefore, often more powerful. It also reminds us that the power of a poem is conveyed in two ways: through its content (what it is saying) and through its format (how it is structured).

Sometimes the subject of a sonnet is—surprise—the sonnet form! Billy Collins, the former poet laureate of the United States (2001–2003), composed this clever sonnet (which had the equally clever name of "Sonnet") on the sonnet form:

> All we need is fourteen lines, well, thirteen now,
> And after this one just a dozen
> To launch a little ship on love's storm-tossed seas,
> Then only ten more left like rows of beans.
> How easily it goes unless you get Elizabethan

Ready-Set-Sonnet!

Keats and his fellow poets used to hold competitions to see who could come up with the best sonnet in just fifteen minutes. Remember: there was no television or iPhone in the nineteenth century. Give it a try. After you've read, say, twenty sonnets, sit down with your notebook and write a sonnet—on any subject—in fifteen minutes. You'll have to choose a form, Italian, Elizabethan, or modern, but that's half the fun.

And insist the iambic bongos must be played
And rhymes positioned at the ends of lines,
One for every station of the cross.
But hang on here while we make the turn
Into the final six where all will be resolved,
Where longing and heartache will find an end,
Where Laura will tell Petrarch to put down his pen,
Take off those crazy medieval tights,
Blow out the lights, and come at last to bed.

As in the ancient love poem "Istanbul 2461," "Sonnet" is another poem leading us to bed. Is a pattern emerging?

Also, although Collins claims that "all will be resolved" in "the final six" lines of a sonnet, is that always true? Take another look at Keats's and Allen's sonnets. Do things feel resolved? Has Keats found his permanent feeling of romantic bliss or Allen his long-lost love? Poems can be open-ended emotionally and intellectually: everything doesn't need to be resolved.

The Haiku

A haiku is a Japanese poem consisting of seventeen syllables, arranged in three unrhymed lines of five, seven, and five syllables. It grew out of an earlier and longer form of Japanese poetry, the tanka, a thirty-line poem. In Japan, the three-line haiku found its greatest expression in the poetry of the seventeenth-century Japanese author Matsuo Basho (who was also trained as a samurai, by the

In this painting, Basho, Japan's most celebrated haiku poet, pauses to share a few words with two farmers.

way—just in case you thought poetry was only for wimps).

Writing about the importance for haiku writers to identify with their subjects, Basho once commented, "The object and yourself must become one, and from that feeling of oneness issues your poetry."

The haiku is a deceptively simple poetic form: its limited number of syllables forces poets to express themselves in specific, striking images. These images often offer sensory impressions of a certain scene or object. Reading the haiku, we sense something much greater, a thought or feeling, hiding behind its simple presentation. Think of the tip of an iceberg and everything lying beneath the surface of the water.

As Steve Kowit points out in his book *In the Palm of Your Hand: The Poet's Portable Workshop*, "The haiku is a poem that combines utter simplicity with some larger understanding of the world."

Because it relies often on a specific metaphor, the haiku became a favorite form of a group of poets who pursued Imagism, a poetic style that became particularly popular in America in the early twentieth century. The Imagists did not follow any one poetic format; more than anything, they wanted to present images that were clear and concentrated. Imagist poets include Ezra Pound (the leader of the movement), D. H. Lawrence, Hilda Doolittle (H. D.), William Carlos Williams, and Amy Lowell.

Lowell was a New England poet who used nature images frequently in her poetry, and she excelled at the haiku. Here are three examples of her haikus:

Amy Lowell— Larger Than Life

The American Imagist poet Amy Lowell (1874–1925) once said she believed that "concentration is of the very essence in poetry." She also wrote a biography of John Keats, published in 1925—the same year she won the Pulitzer Prize for her poetry collection *What's O'Clock*. Although she crafted elegant haikus and other delicately beautiful poetry, she was a large woman who enjoyed smoking cigars and using strong language.

Last night it rained.
Now, in the desolate dawn.
Crying of blue jays.

Love is a game—yes?
I think it is a drowning:
Black willows and stars.

Staying in my room,
I thought of the new Spring leaves.
That day I was happy.

Notice that in each haiku, Lowell uses specific images to convey feelings. Is the first haiku simply about the sounds of blue jays—or do the birds' cries, like the rain and the desolate dawn, reflect anything else? Notice the metaphors (the comparisons without using "like" or "as") in the second haiku: love is both "a game" and "a drowning." The final image of "Black willows and stars" creates a specific sense impression that leaves readers with a dark, sad picture that reinforces the speaker's previous claims of love being a game and a drowning. The poet has conveyed an impression through an image.

Free Verse

Breaking a centuries-long tradition, Walt Whitman was the first to write in free verse—poetry that did not follow any set pattern. His approach was considered radical at the

Haiku and You

Using nature as your inspiration, write five haikus. Choose a specific image from nature—a certain tree or bird, a distinct sound or color—and try to build your haiku around it. Through that image, try to impart a specific feeling or idea. And remember the format: seventeen syllables arranged in three lines of five, seven, and five syllables.

time. "I have found the law of my own poems," he once proclaimed. Despite their often inventive forms, his free-verse poems have their own rhythms. And poets take note: like many accomplished and aspiring poets, he always kept a notebook handy!

In Whitman's "A Noiseless Patient Spider," we can see that—despite the absence of rhyme or standardized line length—the poet has created a specific rhythm.

> A noiseless patient spider,
> I mark'd where on a little promontory it stood isolated,
> Mark'd how to explore the vacant vast surrounding,
> It launch'd forth filament, filament, filament, out of itself,
> Ever unreeling them, ever tirelessly speeding them.

Whitman's poem also offers a valuable lesson in effective word choice. Notice how he uses repeating sounds to create rhythm within the poem: "patient spider," "vacant vast," "forth filament, filament, filament." Also, by repeating the word *filament*, the poet imitates the action of the spider, spinning out its threads. The form is free—there is no set rhyme or line length—but the sound and the force of the words are poetic.

Whitman's short poem illustrates how successful poetry—in any form—uses sound and form to reflect meaning. In the next chapter, we'll look at some of the language tools poets use to express themselves in their poetry.

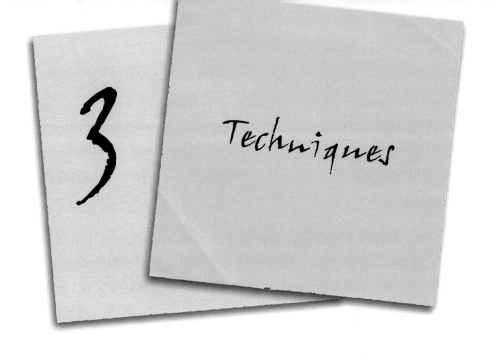

3 Techniques

"WE MURDER TO DISSECT." THE BRITISH poet William Wordsworth once made this astute comment about what happens when we pull things apart to understand them—and he made it in a poem!

Students sometimes feel that English teachers dissect literature too much and require students to take it apart to understand it. Yet, even the most free-form poetry often has a structure, and poets take specific approaches to create each poem. Remember Yeats's comment about the "stitching and unstitching" that goes into writing poetry? Let's take a look at some of the nuts and bolts of what makes a poem a poem. And we'll try not to kill the frog along the way.

Language

The main ingredient of all poetry is, naturally, language. American author Ralph Waldo Emerson once observed,

Poetry

"Language is fossil poetry." For poets, however, the poetry in language is still alive and kicking—not fossilized or dead. In poetry writers use language to describe moods, paint pictures, capture sensation, express ideas, and maybe even touch or change lives.

Those who are drawn to poetry are also drawn to language. Try to focus on the difference between the language you use every day and the language of poetry, and you'll notice that poetic language is simply more condensed. It involves using language in a precise way. Good poetry involves no excess. Also, whereas everyday language communicates information, poetic language often conveys experience.

In addition to being exact and concentrated, the language of poetry is also organized. Poets usually choose a specific form because they believe that it is best suited to what they are trying to express. Let's look at four important tools for writing poetry: line, meter, figures of speech, and imagery.

Line

Lines are the first structural element in a poem. The scholar M. H. Abrams defines a line as "a sequence of words printed as a separate entity on a page." When composing a poem, you must determine how long you want each line to be—and, more importantly, why you want to use a certain line length. Even if you vary line lengths, you must still ask yourself why you have chosen to do so.

The next question to consider is how each line ends and why it ends as it does. Does it end in a rhyme? Does it end in a punctuation mark? Are you even using punctuation marks? Is it an open-ended line that proceeds in thought into the next line?

Here are the opening lines from one of Dickinson's most famous poems:

> Because I could not stop for Death,
> He kindly stopped for me. . . .

Emily Dickinson is arguably the best-known American female poet in history.

Breakdown

Let's look again at Blake's poem "Eternity" and see what happens if we write it as prose instead of poetry: "He who binds to himself a joy does the winged life destroy; but he who kisses the joy as it flies lives in eternity's sunrise." We seem to race over the words on our way to the end of the thought. By breaking the two main thoughts into four lines, Blake compels the reader to pay attention to each line. Think of how much more force the line "Does the winged life destroy" has because it stands alone. It also emphasizes the repeating *d* sounds in the line.

British poet William Blake had a fierce control of language; so much of the power of his poetry lies in how he broke the words into lines.

Now, she could have chosen to combine the two lines into one line: "Because I could not stop for Death, he kindly stopped for me." What does she gain instead by ending the first line with "Death" and beginning the next with "He"? Dickinson usually employed short lines. The elliptical, or condensed, quality of her lines is one of her great gifts to poetry.

Now, let's look at the first three lines from T. S. Eliot's poem "The Love Song of J. Alfred Prufrock":

> Let us go then, you and I,
> When the evening is spread out against the sky
> Like a patient etherized upon a table. . . .

Notice all the choices Eliot made in only the first three lines of his long poem (131 lines!). The first line is relatively short, directed at the reader, and ends on the stressed word "I." It pulls the reader immediately into the poem. The second line, which rhymes with the first, runs into the third without any punctuation and leads the reader directly into the simile in which the evening is compared to "a patient etherized upon a table."

In many poems, lines are gathered into groups known as stanzas. Each stanza is set off by a space in the printed text. Think of stanzas as units of poetry—like verses in a song. As you read more poems, consider why certain lines are gathered into specific stanzas. How does it affect sound? meaning? rhythm? In his book *Why Poetry Matters*, Jay Parini notes that "the formal patterns of poetry

Enjambment

The running of one line into the next with no punctuation at the end of a line is called enjambment. Enjambment can add force and speed to your poetry, as in this stanza by Emily Dickinson:

> The Brain—is wider than the sky—
> For—put them side by side—
> The one the other will contain
> With ease—and you beside—

One line spills into the next, aided by Dickinson's use of dashes to keep the reader moving.

help us to order our lives, to make sense of our lives."

Looking at Cummings's "when serpents bargain for the right to squirm," consider line length and stanza breaks. There are fourteen lines. How are they separated? Count the syllables in each line. What happens in the last two lines? Does any of this look or sound familiar? Language and lines of poetry can be deceptive when they don't look the way we expect them to look.

Notice also that Cummings creates enjambment. Thoughts and observations do not stop abruptly at the end of each line: instead, they spill from one line into the next. Consider what is gained by flowing thoughts openly from line to line. Creating poetry involves making decisions—just like those Cummings made.

Meter or Rhythm

English, like many languages, has its own rhythms. These rhythms occur because of the stress (the hard beats) we put on certain syllables when we speak. When this rhythm is gathered into a regular pattern of stresses, it becomes meter. Listen closely to the rhythms of speech—to those beats—to find natural patterns that you can use when crafting poetry. Rhythm creates the music in a poem.

Using rhythm or meter effectively can also aid the meaning and impact of your poem. Take another look at Cummings's "when serpents bargain for the right to squirm." Full rhymes involve repeating vowel and closing consonant sounds. Notice that Cummings creates

Punctuation— Why Bother?

The American poet E. E. Cummings (1894–1962) hated technology and celebrated all things natural in his writings. He was an inventive writer who used little punctuation, often removed spaces between words, even combined words into new words, and often used capitalization in a nonstandard way. In other words, he wrote as if he were chatting online! Here's a poem on one of his least favorite subjects: the dehumanization of modern humanity.

"when serpents bargain for the right to squirm"

when serpents bargain for the right to squirm
and the sun strikes to gain a living wage—
when thorns regard their roses with alarm
and rainbows are insured against old age

when every thrush may sign no new moon in
if all screech-owls have not okayed his voice
—and any wave signs on the dotted line
or else an ocean is compelled to close

when the oak begs permission of the birch
to make an acorn—valleys accuse their
mountains of having altitude—and march
denounces april as a saboteur

then we'll believe in that incredible
unanimal mankind(and not until)

at dusk #
just when
the Light is filled with birds .)
seriously   i (l.c.)
i begin

to climb the best hill,
driven by black wine.
a village does not move behind
my eyes

the windmills are
silent
their flattened arms
complain steadily against the ~~west.~~

one Clock dimly cries
nine, i stride among the vines
(my heart pursues
against the little moon

a here and then lark
                    who; rises,

and; droops
as if upon a thread invisible)

A graveyard dreams through its
Cluttered and brittle emblems, or
a field (and; pause among
the smell of minute mown lives) oh

my spirit you
tumble
climb and mightily; fatally

i remark how through deep sifted
fields Oxen distinctly move, a
yellowandbluish cat (perched why
Cunningly at this) windows; yes

As with any type of writing, poets write and revise. Here is a manuscript page of "No Thanks 51" marked with E. E. Cummings's revisions.

an "almost rhyme" by repeating only the closing consonant sound of certain words: "squirm" and "alarm," "birch"
and "march." How does this affect the poem's rhythm—
especially when you read it aloud?

Here's a poem written by the African-American poet
Langston Hughes in 1932:

"I, Too"

I, too, sing America.

I am the darker brother.
They send me to eat in the kitchen
When company comes,
But I laugh
And eat well,
And grow strong.

Tomorrow,
I'll be at the table
When company comes.
Nobody'll dare
Say to me,
"Eat in the kitchen,"
Then.

Besides,
They'll see how beautiful I am
And be ashamed—

I, too, am America.

Langston Hughes was an African-American poet and short-story writer whose language echoed that of his community.

Notice the short lines and the breaks in sentences. Hughes creates rhythm by choosing certain words *and* by ending each line in a specific place. Note also how rhythm is created by repeating the first line at the end of the poem and by repeating "When company comes" twice, in mid-stanza.

The language seems not only condensed but also measured. The speaker is waiting, yet he is sure: "But I laugh

To Rhyme or Not to Rhyme

Until the mid–nineteenth century, most poetry was formal: it had a specific meter—a rhythm based on a repeated use of stressed beats—and most of it rhymed. The American poet Robert Frost wrote only formal poetry. Frost would not use free verse; he said it was "too much like playing tennis without the net." Some poets—like some athletes—simply like the challenge!

/ And eat well, / And grow strong." The rhythm has an almost cyclical quality as it rolls the reader back eventually to the first line. Also, whereas "and" would normally not be a stressed word, Hughes adds emphasis by placing it at the beginning of two lines.

A lesson worth learning: line placement and rhythm can compel your reader to listen more carefully and can lend your words more force and color.

Figures of Speech

Figurative language is different from the standard language we use every day. Figures of speech (sometimes called tropes) may be defined as a way of saying one thing and meaning another. It is language that cannot be taken literally. "He eats like a pig" and "I could eat a horse" are examples of figurative language. It would take an entire book to cover all the figures of speech, so let's focus on a few major ones.

Simile and Metaphor

A simile is a comparison between two extremely different things using the word "like" or "as." Consider the Scottish poet Robert Burns's simple statement, "O, my love is like a red, red rose," or Shakespeare's somewhat more negative assertion, "My mistress' eyes are nothing like the sun," or Bob Dylan's lament, "She breaks just like a little girl." Reading these similes compels the reader/listener to grasp the comparison the poet is trying to make. Similes are more direct than their counterpart, metaphors.

The Power of Similes

Similes can be quite powerful when used in the right poetic hands. Here's Langston Hughes's most famous poem, "Dream Deferred." Notice how the use of simile reinforces his message and leads us inexorably toward that last line:

"Dream Deferred"

What happens to a dream deferred?

Does it dry up
Like a raisin in the sun?
Or fester like a sore—
And then run?

Does it stink like rotten meat?

Or crust and sugar over—

Like a syrupy sweet?

Maybe it just sags

Like a heavy load.

Or does it explode?

Metaphors make a similar comparison—but without using any comparative words. They do not say that one thing is *like* another; instead, they say or imply that one thing *is* another.

In his poem "The Voice of the Ancient Bard," Blake's line "Folly is an endless maze"—even standing alone by itself—makes us pause to consider how "folly" (or foolishness) is like a maze. Or, consider Romeo's remark about Juliet in the balcony scene of Shakespeare's *Romeo and Juliet* (act 2, scene 2): "But soft! What light through yonder window breaks? / It is the East, and Juliet is the sun!" Romeo doesn't say Juliet is like the sun—he says she is the sun.

Take a look at Emily Dickinson's poem "Apparently with no surprise" in the sidebar: Who or what is the poet calling a "blonde Assassin"—and why? How is the phrase used as a metaphor, and how does it emphasize the point of Dickinson's poem?

Metonymy and Synecdoche

Metaphors come in different shapes and sizes. Two more useful ones to know are metonymy and synecdoche. Metonymy occurs when the writer replaces the name of one thing with something closely related. For example, when a newscaster says that "the White House issued a statement today," he is using metonymy. "The White House" refers to the president or the president's press secretary. Referring to executives as "suits" is another example of metonymy. The executives' manner of dress in this case represents everything about them.

Blonde Assassin— Punk Rocker?

It may sound like the name of a rock group, but "blonde Assassin" appears in a poem by Emily Dickinson. The phrase offers an excellent lesson in the use of metaphor:

> Apparently with no surprise
>
> To any happy Flower
>
> The Frost beheads it at its play—
>
> In accidental power—
>
> The blonde Assassin passes on—
>
> That Sun proceeds unmoved
>
> To measure off another Day
>
> For an Approving God.

Synecdoche occurs when writers use a part of something to represent the whole. When they call for "all hands on deck" on a ship, they obviously mean the sailors attached to those hands. When you tell your friend that you like her new "wheels" and you mean her new car, you are using synecdoche. The wheels represent the entire car—unless you're just admiring her hubcaps.

Personification

In personification, an object, animal, or abstract concept is referred to in human terms. When John Donne proclaims, "Death, be not proud," he personifies Death by granting it the human characteristic of pride. When the blues singer Billie Holiday sang the lyrics, "Good morning, heartache, / Sit down," she was addressing her grief as a person she had to meet every morning. As these examples indicate, poets use personification to project human emotions and traits onto inanimate objects, ideas, or animals.

In "The Love Song of J. Alfred Prufrock," T. S. Eliot describes "The yellow fog that rubs its back upon the window panes" and "Licked its tongue into the corners of the evening." The poet personifies the fog by giving it the ability to rub and to lick. In "To Autumn," John Keats, speaking about the season of fall, calls it the "Close bosom-friend of the maturing sun." Throughout his sonnets, Shakespeare personifies the abstract concepts of Time and Death by referring to them with masculine pronouns (him, his).

Imagery

Imagery may be defined as sense perception referred to in a poem or other literary work. Sights, sounds, smells, tastes, and textures—all come alive in the images of good writers. Poets often seem to have heightened senses: they are acutely aware of the world around them, of its many images, and they know how to convey those images in language.

Let's return to the haiku writer Basho's comment about a poet becoming one with the object. This is one way to keep focus on specific images, and that advice can certainly extend to poems other than haikus. Consider one of the most famous poems in the English language, "The Red Wheelbarrow," written in 1923 by the American poet William Carlos Williams. Although not a haiku, it displays the same intense focus and offers a powerful lesson in the importance of imagery.

"The Red Wheelbarrow"

so much depends
upon
a red wheel
barrow

glazed with rain
water

beside the white
chickens.

Imagery in Williams's poems includes colors (red, white), touch (glazed, water), and the main visual image of the wheelbarrow next to some chickens. The poet stresses the importance of these images by beginning his poem, "So much depends / upon. . . ."—and by giving "upon" its own line. But, *what* depends upon this seemingly trivial image? The poet opens the poem up to readers to either interpret what they think "depends upon" the images—or to bring their own responses to the imagery.

William Carlos Williams, caricatured here by Eva Herrmann, was both a physician and a poet, and each of his disciplines informed the other.

The poems of Ofelia Zepeda reflect her life, and that of other American Indians in the American culture.

Native Images

The American Indian poet Ofelia Zepeda is also a linguistics professor. Her poems reflect the lives of her people, the Tohono O'odham, a desert-dwelling tribe. Note how her poetry focuses on everyday images in "Pulling Down the Clouds":

With dreams of a distant noise disturbing his sleep,

the smell of dirt, wet, for the first time in what seemed

like months.

The change in the molecules is sudden, they enter

The nasal cavity.

He contemplates the smell, what is that smell?

It is rain.

Rain somewhere out in the desert.

Comforted in this knowledge he turns over and

continues his sleep,

Dreams of women with harvesting sticks

Raised to the sky.

Song Lyrics

Song lyrics can also offer fine examples of imagery. The Oklahoma-born singer-songwriter Jimmy Webb is the only composer to have won Grammy Awards for music, lyrics, and orchestration (as of 2010). Since the late 1960s, his thoughtful and imagery-laden lyrics have captivated millions of listeners. Here are the lyrics to his song "The Moon's a Harsh Mistress," about an impossible love that remains out of reach. Webb took the title of this song from a science fiction novel by Robert Heinlein.

Notice Webb's clever use of imagery throughout. You'll also find metaphor, simile, and personification. See if you can spot them!

"The Moon's a Harsh Mistress"

See her as she flies
Golden sails across the skies
Close enough to touch
But careful if you try
Though she looks as warm as gold
The moon's a harsh mistress
The moon can be so cold

Once the sun did shine
And Lord it felt so fine
The moon a phantom rose
Through the mountains and the pine

And then the darkness fell
The moon's a harsh mistress
It's hard to love her well

I fell out of her eyes
I fell out of her heart
I fell down on my face
I tripped and I missed my star
I fell and fell alone

The moon's a harsh mistress
The sky is made of stone
The moon's a harsh mistress
She's hard to call your own.

Now you have more ammunition in your arsenal to write poetry (a bad metaphor—in case you didn't notice!). Other than hard work, the most important thing is simply to read as much poetry as possible. Read all kinds of poetry, from the most structured to the loosest in form. Read different styles by different poets.

Read poems from all eras and from all over the world: you'll be surprised to find similarities among their subject matter and themes. The more you read, the more you will become attuned to the importance of the sound of poetry—how words are chosen as much for sound as they are for meaning. And don't forget that all the living and the reading you do will feed into your poetry if you pay attention (and maybe even take notes!).

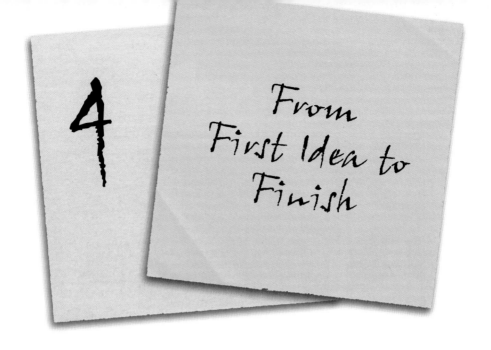

4
From First Idea to Finish

THE EIGHTEENTH-CENTURY POET Alexander Pope wrote in his poem "Sound and Sense," "True ease in writing comes from art, not chance, / As those move easiest who have learned to dance." That's a simile, right? It's not luck, claims Pope, it's skill.

In the previous chapter you learned some of the basic steps for writing poetry. Now, it's time to take those "dance lessons" and apply them. And that, my friends, is an extended metaphor, carried throughout this paragraph.

In his book *In the Palm of Your Hand: The Poet's Portable Workshop*, Steve Kowit observes, "Writers spend a lot of time at their writing because it gives them pleasure." For those of us who love words, writing is a pleasure. Like anything else you do, the better you become, the more you enjoy doing it—and the same holds true for poetry.

How do poets write? When the American poet Theodore Roethke faced a problem in his writing, he would go

This drawing by Aubrey Beardsley depicts "The Battle of the Beaux and Belles" in Alexander Pope's poem, "The Rape of the Lock."

to bed until he solved the problem—and then get up and start writing again. The Roman poet Virgil used to walk through his garden all day long just to come up with a single line of poetry—and he considered that a good day at work. Different poets write differently.

We return to Yeats's comment about the "stitching and unstitching" that goes into writing poetry that appears to flow smoothly. In poetry, as with any other form of writing, good writing is in the rewriting.

Keep a Journal

If it was good enough for Walt Whitman, it's good enough for you. A journal can be your private space, a place to express ideas, observations, and feelings. You can also put photographs, drawings, newspaper clippings, your favorite poems, song lyrics, and personal letters into your journal. Whatever moves you or inspires you or gets your creative juices flowing. Remember: inspiration can come from anywhere. Save it in a journal.

Make a List

Where to begin? Make a list of subjects you'd like to turn into poems: a wonderful or terrible experience; an idea about life that you believe in strongly; a feeling you once had that you have never shared; the first time you realized you were no longer a child; a moment in nature—on a beach, in a forest—and your strongest sense impressions of it; your feelings about romance, friendship, betrayal, family. Write poems about subjects that matter to you.

Maybe a poem in this book caught your attention—maybe the one about the wheelbarrow or one of the haikus by the cigar-smoking Imagist Amy Lowell. Jot down some thoughts on how it makes you feel or your reaction to it. This, too, can be the beginning of your own poem.

Perhaps you can take the last line of a poem you like and use it as the first line of your own. See where it leads you—let it inspire you to take the line to places the original poet would never have imagined.

Choose Your Subject

Your own life may well be the best source of inspiration for your poetry. Think about your strongest childhood memory, your secret affection for someone, the greatest betrayal you have known, an experience that left you speechless. You don't have to be old to write good poetry—you simply need to be aware and expressive.

Anyone can write. One very important hint to the beginning writer: Be specific!

Be specific. Where will "I'm going to write about love" take you? Into a large open field strewn with unfinished poems and bad pop songs. Instead, narrow your focus: "I'm going to write about what it feels like to love someone I can never have." Don't write a poem about war—write a poem about a soldier's anxiety when he first says good-bye to his wife and child or the tension between a soldier's personal value system and his orders to kill.

In her book *The Discovery of Poetry*, Frances Mayes suggests, "Write poems that matter very much to you, whether they are memories of childhood, meditations, or sound experiments. The quality of deep feeling, thought, or intense energy will guarantee that your poem, at least, has life."

Who's Your Speaker?

A poem is first and foremost a work of art. That means that we'll never really know whether the poet is the speaker in a poem or has simply created a voice or character who is speaking. Maybe Emily Dickinson never stopped for anyone (let alone Death). Maybe she just thought it was a clever way to express her feelings about loss. Maybe Keats never stared at a star and thought about anything. Maybe he just felt that addressing a star in his sonnet was a good way to get out his feelings about the passage of time.

Don't confuse the speaker in a poem with the author. The speaker may simply be a creation of the author's imagination. The "I" of your poem does not necessarily have to be you. You can become anyone.

The Subject Is Poetry

What's the proper subject for a poem?
Any subject is appropriate for a poem!
These titles of some recent anthologies of
poetry offer a glimpse into the diverse
topics that poets address in their writing:

Rubber Side Down: The Biker Poet Anthology
Taste: An Anthology of Poetry about Food
Kindness: A Vegetarian Poetry Anthology

What's the Story?

The Welsh poet Dylan Thomas defined poetry as "the rhythmic, inevitably narrative, movement from an over-clothed blindness to a naked vision." There's usually a story—a narrative—lurking behind a poem. Decide what your story is and who's telling it.

"Even when I'm writing a poem," said the modern American author Raymond Carver, "I'm still trying to tell a story." Take a look at Carver's poem "Happiness." That may seem like a worn-out subject for a poem. As you read the poem, notice how Carver tells a story about something he saw to express emotion.

"Happiness"

So early it's still almost dark out.
I'm near the window with coffee,
and the usual morning stuff
that passes for thought.

When I see the boy and his friend
walking up the road
to deliver the newspaper.

They wear caps and sweaters,
and the one boy has a bag over his shoulder.
They are so happy
they aren't saying anything, these boys.

"Even when I'm writing a poem," says Raymond Carver, "I'm still trying to tell a story." A poem is a way to tell a story in a more concentrated, emotion-laden form.

I think if they could, they would take
each other's arm.
It's early in the morning,
and they are doing this thing together.

They come on, slowly.
The sky is taking on light,
though the moon still hangs pale over the water.

Such beauty that for a minute
death and ambition, even love,
doesn't enter into this.

Happiness. It comes on
unexpectedly. And goes beyond, really,
Any early morning talk about it.

Choose Your Form

Decide whether a specific form is best for what you want
to say, or if a free-form, open poem better suits your purpose. Write a poem both ways—one that has rhythm and
rhyme and one that does not—and listen to the difference.
Which works better for your subject matter? You'll hear it.

Remember that if you choose to write a free-verse or
open poem, it may still have rhythm and rhyme. However,
it will not follow any specific pattern. Lines should not be
all the same length, with the same number of syllables.
Remember to read aloud as you write: if it doesn't sound
right, it probably isn't.

Perhaps the subject of your poem will be suited to a particular form. One of the reasons Shakespeare's plays have become immortal is that iambic pentameter has a natural rhythm that "sounds" like regular spoken English. It's memorable: it sticks to the crevices of your brain (a bad metaphor; I admit it). Yet, he gained intensity by writing so many of his plays in verse—in a specific poetic form. The same can be said for the sonnet and the haiku.

Write with Force

Choose your words carefully; find the words that say the most. The eighteenth-century British author Samuel Johnson once said, "Words too familiar, or too remote, defeat the purpose of a poet." When choosing your words, struggle not to write in a pretentious language you think sounds "poetic." At the same time, a poem isn't a grocery list (now, there's an interesting starting point for a poem!)—enliven your language beyond the ordinary.

The condensed quality of poetic language is also its strength. It may be painful, but cut whatever words are unnecessary—even if it hurts. You'll know you're there (or close to it) when there's nothing left to take away.

Also, write with color: make sure your words are lively and forceful. Choose words that evoke a response—words that will move, touch, or even anger your reader. Be specific. Find those images that express what you are trying to say without having to tell the reader directly.

Think in Pictures

The American author Ernest Hemingway, who was also a journalist, claimed that he got inspiration from artists and composers as well as from other writers. "I learned as much from painters about how to write as from writers," he admitted. Find a picture of a Cubist painting by Picasso or a modernist sculpture by Jean Arp or a mobile by Alexander Calder and stare at it until its artistic language speaks to you.

Rewrite and Revise!

Now that you've written your first poem, set aside your first draft for a while and then return to it. How does it sound? Are the lines ending where they should, or are you pausing in the middle of lines? Maybe where you find yourself pausing is a line break.

Once again, good writing is often in the rewriting. Don't be discouraged because that sonnet didn't just pour out of you (chances are they didn't pour out of Shakespeare, either, and he wrote 154 sonnets that we know of). Rework it and rework it until each line sounds "right" and is appropriate for what you are trying to say.

Revising your work is the best method for getting better and achieving your goals. Read your poems aloud—or have others read them. Listen for what sounds right and what falls flat. Get rid of everything that doesn't work. The caustic American wit Dorothy Parker referred to this process as "killing your babies."

Live Readings

It may sound frightening at first, but reading your poetry aloud is a good way to get feedback and to hear your poetry. Many coffeehouses feature open-mike nights, when anyone can get up for a certain amount of time and play some music or do a reading. Some nights are set aside specifically for poetry. The crowd will be small and intimate—and you may even get some valuable feedback (including compliments!).

Don't Give Up!

You can even make a poem out of your failed efforts. The American poet Sylvia Plath expressed her frustration with writing in a poem called "Stillborn":

These poems do not live: it's a sad diagnosis.

They grew their toes and fingers well enough,

Their little foreheads bulged with concentration.

If they missed out on walking about like people

It wasn't for any lack of mother-love.

O I cannot explain what happened to them!

They are proper in shape and number and every part.

They sit so nicely in the pickling fluid!

They smile and smile and smile at me.

And still the lungs won't fill and the heart won't start.

They are not pigs, they are not even fish—

Though they have a piggy and a fishy air—

It would be better if they were alive, and that's what they were.

But they are dead, and their mother near dead with distraction,

And they stupidly stare and do not speak of her.

Sylvia Plath's life was short, but her poetry is still read and beloved worldwide.

5

Anyone Can Write

Some Exercises

Now, you have a journal and it's full of ideas (or blank pages, but that's okay, too). The poet Anne Sexton once said, "It may take me ten pages of nothing, of terrible writing, and then I'll get a line, and I'll think, 'That's what I mean.'" Don't be discouraged because a poem won't pour out of you. No one takes to the soccer field as a champion: it takes hard work and constant practice.

Here are some exercises to stretch your poetic muscles and to get your creative juices flowing. Remember that one idea may well lead you to another.

1. **Fill in the Simile**. Finish the following similes and try to think in concrete images. Afterward, turn the same similes into metaphors. Try to be original.

The seagull, flying like _____.

Her hair, falling like _____.

The mountains, tall as _____.
That runner, racing like _____.
The shadows, advancing like _____.
Homer's head, round as _____.

2. **Five-Minute Poem**. Choose a subject and write a poem in any length or form in five minutes. When you're done, read it aloud. Then write another poem in five minutes on the same subject. Compare the two poems and decide which is better and why.

3. **Memory Lane**. In your mind, walk through a place you have been that holds special meaning for you—good or bad. Write down everything you can remember about this place in phrases and sense impressions. Afterward, see if there's a poem hiding in there somewhere—or at least an idea for one!

4. **Landscape Painter**. Take your notebook out to a park, a beach, a wood, or a field. Jot down all your observations and sense impressions. Think in terms of colors, shapes, and sound. Turn those impressions into a poem describing that place or your response to it. Paint with words.

5. **Sonnet Stretch**. Write a sonnet about an unlikely subject—one that has nothing to do with love. Choose a political topic, for example: the misuse of power, an institution you don't believe in, a political leader you admire, a hot-button issue you feel strongly about. Express your

opinions within the classic sonnet form—or apply the more modern approach.

6. **Five by Five**. Open a book and choose five words randomly and write them on a piece of paper. Make each word the first word of a new stanza. Try to write a five-stanza poem connecting the five words.

7. **My Poet**. Make a poet your own. Choose a poet whose work you admire or one whose life sounds fascinating. Learn everything you can about that poet and read everything he or she has written. Then write a poem in the poet's style—but try to make it your own.

8. **Desk Haiku**. Choose three objects on your desk at home and write a haiku about each one. Focus on the object and try to condense all your thoughts into the three-line haiku form. Remember Basho's advice about becoming "one" with the object. Convey an *impression* through your *image*.

9. **Attend a Poetry Slam**. A poetry slam is a competition at which poets are given a certain amount of time to read their poetry aloud. They are usually then judged by their audience. It takes strong will and a vibrant personality to read a poem aloud at a slam, but it's a great way to share your poetry. Attend some and see for yourself; they are often held at bookstores and coffeehouses.

Introduction

p. 6, "stitching and unstitching . . .": William Butler Yeats, "Adam's Curse."

Chapter One

p. 11, "These include . . .": For more information on the history of the epic poem, *see* M. H. Abrams, *A Glossary of Literary Terms*, (6th ed., Harcourt Brace Jovanovich, 1993), 53–56.

p. 12, "Istanbul 2461. . .": Sebnem Arsu, "For Valentine's Day, the Oldest Love Poem in the World," *Indian Express* (February 15, 2006), www.indianexpress.com/oldStory/87897/ (accessed January 21, 2010).

Chapter Two

p. 22, "The object . . .": quoted in Steve Kowit, *In the Palm of Your Hand: The Poet's Portable Workshop* (Gardner, ME: Tilbury House, 1995), p. 74.

p. 29, "You're in the city . . .": Dick Allen, "Lost Love," *New Yorker*, June 29, 1987, p. 34.

p. 33, "Poem 2461 appears in *Anthology of American Literature*, vol. 2, *Realism to the Present* (New York: Macmillan, 1989), p. 181.

p. 34, "The Imagists did not . . .": Abrams, p. 88.

p. 35, "concentration is of . . .": quoted in "Biography of Amy Lowell," *Poem Hunter*, www.poemhunter.com/amy-lowell/biography/ (accessed: March 1, 2010).

p. 36, "Last night it rained . . .": Amy Lowell, *What's O'Clock*, (Boston: Houghton Mifflin, 1925), pp. 37–43.

Chapter Three

p. 40, "a sequence of words . . .": Abrams, p. 112.

pp. 44, 46, "the formal patterns . . .": Jay Parini, *Why Poetry Matters* (New Haven, CT: Yale University Press, 2008), p. 100.

p. 52, "too much like . . .": quoted in Parini, p. 108.

p. 59, "The Red Wheelbarrow" appears in *Anthology of American Literature*, vol. 2, *Realism to the Present*, p. 1265.

pp. 61–62, "Pulling Down the Clouds": Ofelia Zepeda, *Ocean Power* (Tucson: University of Arizona Press, 1965).

Chapter Four

pp. 65, 67, "When the American poet . . .": John Timpane and Maureen Watts, *Poetry for Dummies* (New York: Wiley, 2001), p. 144.

p. 69, "Write poems that . . .": Frances Mayes, *The Discovery of Poetry* (San Diego: Harvest, 2001), p. 459.

p. 71, "the rhythmic, inevitably narrative . . .": Kowit, p. 11.

p. 71, "Even when I'm . . .": Raymond Carver, quoted on the Writing University, www.writinguniversity.org/index.php/main/author/raymond_carver/ (accessed April 1, 2010).

p. 75, "I learned as much from . . .": quoted in Jim Walker and Mark Shaw, *The Poetry Report: Creative Ideas and Publishing Strategies for Aspiring Poets* (Aspen, CO: Books for Life Foundation, 2004), p. 184.

Chapter Five

p. 79, "It may take me . . .": Frances Mayes, *The Discovery of Poetry* (San Diego: Harvest, 2001), p. 460.

Books

Kowit, Steve. *In the Palm of Your Hand: The Poet's Portable Workshop*. Gardner, ME: Tilbury House, 1995.

Mehta, Diane. *How to Write Poetry*. New York: Spark, 2008.

Parini, Jay. *Why Poetry Matters*. New Haven, CT: Yale University Press, 2008.

Poetry Center. John Timpane and Maureen Watts.

Poetry for Dummies. New York: Wiley, 2001.

Poetry

American Poems

This website is dedicated to showcasing all the great American poets—both classic and contemporary. It includes information on more than 230 poets and more than 8,000 poems. You'll find sections titled Members, Top Forty Poems, Love Poems, and Poem of the Day.
www.americanpoems.com/

Poetry Daily

This website offers an anthology of contemporary poetry and features a new poem every day. You'll also find articles and information about poetry and poets reading their poems aloud. There is also a news section, a gift shop, and a Twitter link.
www.poems.com/

Poetry Magic

Poetry Magic is a website for poets, aspiring poets, and students of poetry. You'll find sections titled Approaches, Persuasion, Starting Off, and Word Choice. There are also more than ten sections on publishing your work, including one on printing your poems in booklet form (these booklets are called chapbooks).
www.poetrymagic.co.uk/

Poets.org

Run by the Academy of American Poets, this website features poems, essays, interviews, poetry readings, and a discussion forum. A section titled Poetry Near You connects you to poetry events in your state; Poetic Toolbox contains information on poetic movements, forms, and authors. You'll also find a bookstore with CDs and videos. www.poets.org/

All websites were accurate and accessible as of November 4, 2010.

Bibliography

The following is a selection of material the author found helpful in his research.

Abrams, M. H. *A Glossary of Literary Terms*. 6th ed. Fort Worth, TX: Harcourt Brace Jovanovich, 1993.

Alpaugh, David. "The New Math of Poetry." *Chronicle Review* (February 26, 2010), B12–14.

Kowit, Steve. *In the Palm of Your Hand: The Poet's Portable Workshop*. Gardner, ME: Tilbury House, 1995.

Lowell, Amy. *What's O'Clock*. Boston: Houghton Mifflin, 1925.

Mayes, Frances. *The Discovery of Poetry*. San Diego: Harcourt, 2001.

McMichael, George, ed. *Anthology of American Literature.* Vol. 2, *Realism to the Present*, 4th ed. New York: Macmillan, 1989.

Mehta, Diane. *How to Write Poetry*. New York: Spark, 2008.

Parini, Jay. *Why Poetry Matters*. New Haven, CT: Yale University Press, 2008.

Perrine, Laurence. *Sound and Sense: An Introduction to Poetry*. 7th ed. New York: Harcourt Brace Jovanovich, 1987.

Poetry Center. John Timpane and Maureen Watts. *Poetry for Dummies*. New York: Wiley, 2001.

Walker, Jim, and Mark Shaw. *Poetry Report: Creative Ideas and Publishing Strategies for Aspiring Poets*. Aspen, CO: Books for Life Foundation, 2004.

Index

Page numbers in **boldface** are illustrations. Proper names of fictional characters are shown by (C).

Poetry

Poetry

95

About the Author

MARK MUSSARI is a freelance writer, translator, and editor living in Tucson, Arizona. He received his Ph.D. in Scandinavian languages and literature from the University of Washington and taught literature, including poetry, for a number of years at Villanova University. He is the author of many nonfiction books for Marshall Cavendish Benchmark, most recently *Shakespeare's Sonnets* in our Shakespeare Explained series, and *Haruki Murakami* and *Amy Tan* in our Today's Writers and Their Works series. He has also published many academic and consumer magazine articles on art, design, and entertainment.